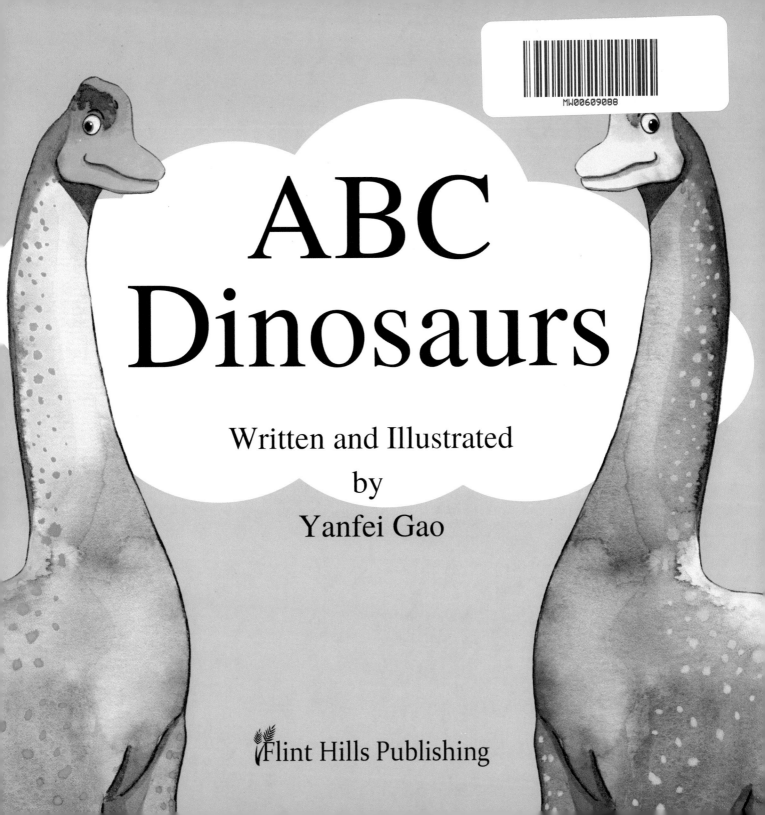

ABC
Dinosaurs

Written and Illustrated

by

Yanfei Gao

Flint Hills Publishing

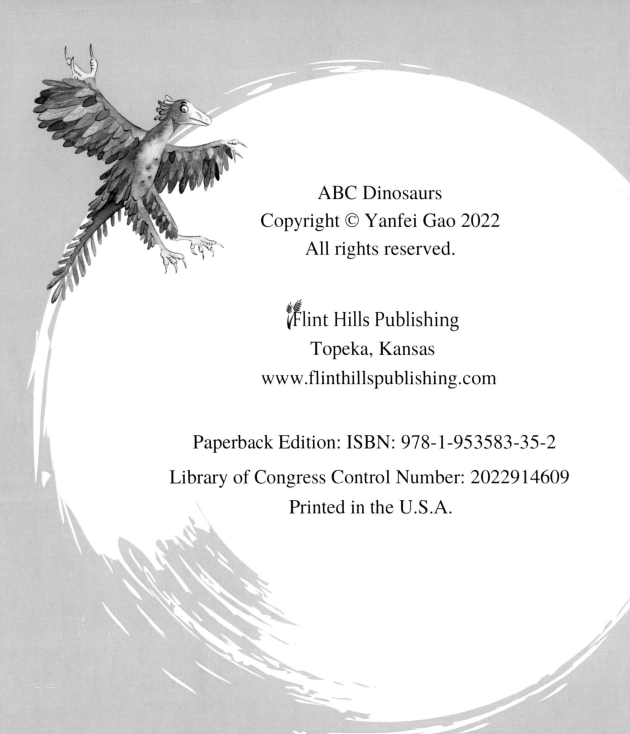

ABC Dinosaurs

Flint Hills Publishing

Topeka, Kansas

www.flinthillspublishing.com

Paperback Edition: ISBN: 978-1-953583-35-2

Library of Congress Control Number: 2022914609

Printed in the U.S.A.

This Book
belongs
to

_____

A

is for **Allosaurus picking apples.**

Say my name: al-oh-SORE-us. My name means "other lizard."

With knife-like teeth and sharp claws, Allosaurus was the most fearsome hunter of the Jurassic period.

Fun Fact: How can you tell Allosaurus apart from T-Rex? Allosaurus has three fingers on each hand, while T-Rex has only two.

B

This well-known dinosaur held her head high to eat the leaves of tall tree-like plants.

Fun Fact: Brachiosaurus gets her name from her arm bones, which are taller than most people.

is for Brachiosaurus blowing bubbles.

Say my name: Cryo-loaf-oh-SORE-us
My name means "frozen crested
lizard."

C

Cryolophosaurus ruled Antarctica in the Jurassic Period. Instead of a crown, she had a bony crest on her head.

Fun Fact:

Dinosaurs in Antarctica? Yes! Antarctica was much warmer when dinosaurs walked the earth.

is for Cryolophosaurus cuddling with cats.

This small plant eater had armor built into her skin!

Fun Fact:

Today, crocodiles have bony armor in their skin, similar to Dracopelta.

is for Dracopelta eating donuts.

Say my name: i-nee-oh-SORE-us.
My name means "buffalo lizard."

A cousin of the famous Triceratops. Einiosaurus had a nose horn that curved forward, not backward.

Fun Fact:

Einiosaurus was easy to spot—no other horned dinosaur had a nose horn like hers!

is for Einiosaurus hiding Easter eggs.

Say my name: fab-roh-SORE-us.
I am named after the French
scientist Jean Henri Fabre.

This was one of the earliest dinosaurs. He lived in what is now Africa during the late Triassic Period.

Fun Fact: Fabrosaurus had five fingers on each hand— just like most people!

F is for Fabrosaurus making a fire.

This dinosaur ate plants AND meat. She was an omnivore. With long legs and hollow bones, Gallimimus was built for running.

Fun Fact: Many scientists think Gallimimus was the fastest dinosaur—even faster than a racehorse!

is for Gallimimus going to the grocery store.

H

This duck-billed dinosaur roamed the woodlands of North America, eating plants.

Fun Fact:

Unlike ducks, Hadrosaurus had lots of teeth in the back of his mouth. He needed them to chew the tough plants he loved to eat.

is for Hadrosaurus on Halloween.

Her thumbs were spikes that helped to protect her from the fierce meat-eaters of the Cretaceous Period.

Fun Fact:

Early scientits made a big mistake when putting the first Iguanodon skeleton together —they put her spiky thumb on her nose!

is for Iguanodon ice skating.

Say my name: jak-sahr-toh-SORE-us.
My name means " lizard of
the Jaxartes River."

The large crest on the Jaxartosaurus' head looked like a helmet.

Fun Fact: Jaxartosaurus may have used his crest like a musical instrument to call to his friends and family.

J is for **Jaxartosaurus** making jelly beans.

K

This well-armored cousin of Stegosaurus had spikes coming out of his shoulders.

Fun Fact:

Kentrosaurus might not have done well in school—his brain was the size of a walnut.

is for Kentrosaurus paddling a kayak.

is for Lambeosaurus doing laundry.

Say my name: lam-bee-oh-SORE-us.
I am named after the paleontologist
Lawrence Morris Lambe.

Another dinosaur with a bony crest on her head, the Lambeosaurus' crest was nearly as big as the rest of her skull.

Fun Fact:

Most adult humans have 32 teeth. Lambeosaurus had more than 100!

Microraptor looked a bit like a bird, but she had feathers on her arms and her legs.

Fun Fact:

Microraptor couldn't exactly fly, but she could glide from tree to tree. Today's birds are related to Microraptor. Birds are the only dinosaurs still alive today.

M is for **Microraptor** doing magic tricks.

N

Noasaurus lived with giants like the long-necked Argentinosaurus, but Noasaurus was tiny—tiny for a dinosaur anyway.

Fun Fact: Dinosaurs that eat meat, like Noasaurus, are called carnivores.

N is for Noasaurus dancing the Nutcracker.

Don't be fooled
by her toothless
beak—Oviraptor
ate both plants
and meat.

Fun Fact:

Scientists were
wrong to call
Oviraptors "egg
thieves" just
because they found
Oviraptor fossils
with fossil eggs. In
fact, Oviraptors
were great parents
—they sat on their
eggs just like birds
do today.

is for   viraptor racing an ostrich.

Say my name: pak-ee-SEF-uh-lo-SORE-us. My name means "thick-headed lizard."

P

This dinosaur had a very, very thick skull. Pachycephalosaurus likely fought with each other by butting heads—like mountain goats do today.

Fun Fact:

Talk about a bone head! Pachycephalosaurus' skull was about 20 times thicker than most other animals her size.

is for Pachycephalosaurus making a pizza.

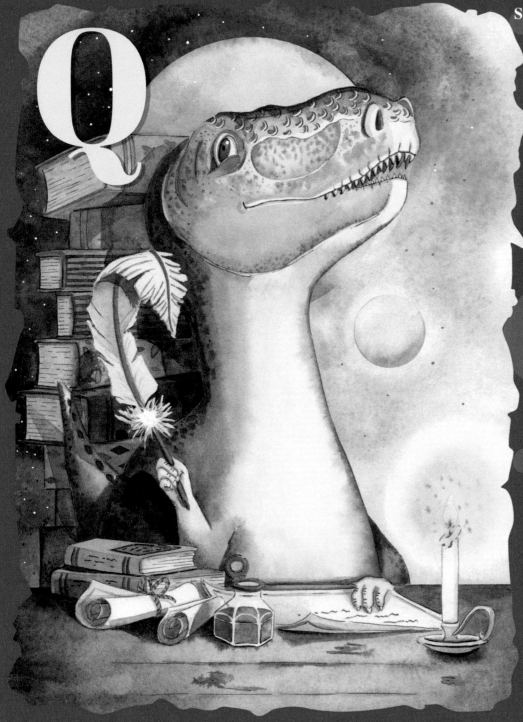

Say my name: kwil-me-SORE-us.
I am named after the Quilme
people of South America.

Quilmesaurus was a meat-eating dinosaur that lived in South America. Dinosaur fossils have been found all over the world!

Fun Fact: Quilmesaurus belonged to a group of dinosaurs called "theropods." Theropods walked on two legs and most ate meat— like the famous T-Rex.

Q is for **Quilmesaurus** writing with a quill.

R

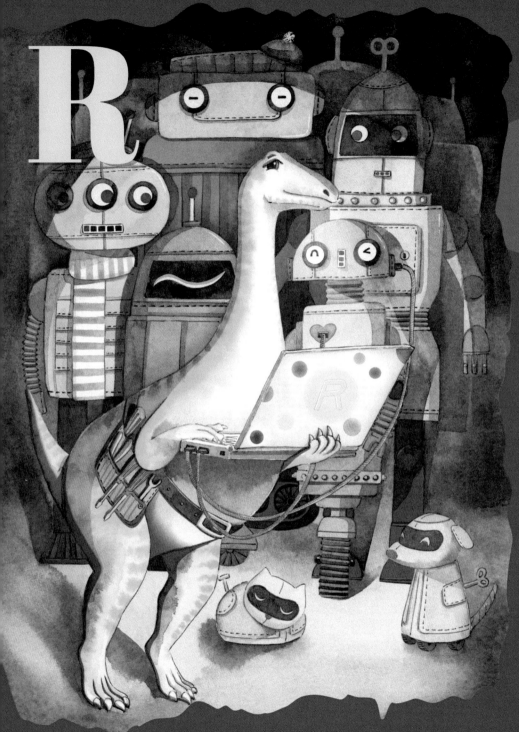

Say my name: re-o-ha-SORE-us.
I am named after La Rioja
Province in Argentina.

She was one of the earliest dinosaurs, with a small head, long neck, and long tail. The feet of Riojasaurus were like elephant feet— but with claws!

Fun Fact: Plant-eating dinosaurs like Riojasaurus sometimes ate small stones to help them digest their dinners.

is for Riojasaurus fixing robots.

This dinosaur had a long, narrow skull, like a crocodile. She also had webbed feet, like a duck. Spinosaurus spent a lot of time in rivers catching fish.

Fun Fact:

Spinosaurus was even bigger than T-Rex. She is the biggest meat-eating dinosaur that scientists have discovered so far!

is for   pinosaurus scared by spiders.

is for T-Rex inviting Triceratops to tea.

T-Rex and Triceratops might be the best known dinosaurs of all. T-Rex is short for Tyrannosaurus Rex. It had a huge skull and a bone-crushing bite. **Say my name: tie-RAN-oh-sore-us-REKS. My name means "tyrant lizard king."** Triceratops had an even bigger skull and three dangerous horns on her face. **Say my name: tri-CERA-tops. My name means "three-horned face."**

Fun Fact:

Triceratops and T-Rex really did live together in the Cretaceous Period, but they weren't friends. Some Triceratops fossils even have T-Rex tooth marks on them!

Utahraptor wasn't the biggest meat-eating dinosaur, but his combination of speed, smarts, and sharp claws made him one of the best hunters around.

Fun Fact:

The large, curving claws on Utahraptor's hind feet were almost a foot long!

is for Utahraptor playing the ukulele.

She was one of the smallest dinosaurs—only about the size of a turkey!

Fun Fact:

For her small size, Velociraptor had a huge brain. Scientists think she was one of the smartest dinosaurs.

is for Velociraptor the veterinarian.

Say my name: wan-nan-oh-SORE-us. I am named after the place I was discovered in China.

Do you have a little cousin? Wannanosaurus is kind of like Triceratops' little cousin.

Fun Fact:

Dinosaurs that eat plants, like Wannanosaurus, are called herbivores.

is for Wannanosaurus growing watermelons.

X

Say my name: zee-no-CERA-tops. My name means "alien horned face."

Another Triceratops cousin, she has spikes coming from everywhere.

Fun Fact: Even though she has a beak like a parrot, Xenoceratops is not closely related to birds.

is for Xenoceratops playing the xylophone.

Say my name: YIN-long.
My name means "hidden dragon."

Not all dinosaurs were giants. Yinlong was an herbivore. He hid in the shadows and ate plants.

Fun Fact: This dinosaur actually lived like today's sheep. He browsed on plants growing close to the ground.

is for Yinlong doing yoga.

Say my name: zoo-CHENG-go-sore-us.
I am named after the Zhucheng
Region in China.

Duckbilled dinosaurs are called hadrosaurs. Zhuchengosaurus was one of the biggest!

Fun Fact:

A paleontologist is a scientist who studies dinosaurs. You can be a paleontologist! Believe in yourself and you can do anything!

is for Zhuchengosaurus the zookeeper.

Dinosaurs are fun! Let's read the book again.

Made in the USA
Monee, IL
21 November 2022

18264206R00019